UNDERSTANDING TRUMP

FROM BOTH SIDES OF THE WALL

MICHAEL GREENWOOD

KDM PUBLISHERS

INTRODUCTION

Welcome to the year 2017, where Donald Trump is president! This is the year of controversy and strife. This is indeed a time where battles are constantly afoot, and where no opinion can be voiced and not get attacked by someone, somewhere. Ordinary people exist in a state of despair about how to move forward, and about how to get past the hatred; about how to find peace, love, and understanding in a world that constantly seems to be on a knife edge.

So how is that done? Well, this book has information from both sides of "the wall." By being able to see the other point of view, it can become easier to find acceptance and an understanding that there is more than one way of seeing things. It seems ever more common for a mere opinion to be taken as a cold hard fact. That is simply not the truth. An opinion is just that. An opinion. Just because someone believes in something, it does not make it true. Nor does it mean that the person behind the opinion is evil.

After reading this book, you will hopefully walk away with a better understanding of what resides on the other side of the wall to you. This will help you get along better with people of different political affiliations. If you still struggle to understand that other side, then try another reading of this book! The important thing is to understand. That is the key to harmony.

Read this book to truly understand the opposing side of your political affiliation. Then, go out and educate others on the importance of understanding opposing views.

UNDERSTANDING TRUMP

I don't do it for the money. I've got enough, much more than I'll ever
need. I do it to do it. Deals are my art form.

— DONALD TRUMP

a lot of people criticize the president and his choices, simply
because they do not understand what goes into being the
president. There is really no presidential user manual on what is right
or wrong. This should be obvious, given that every president has
governed the country differently than his predecessors. However, it
seems that many expect Donald Trump to govern the US exactly like
Barack Obama did before him, which is an absurd expectation.
Obama was a democratic president, and Trump is a Republican one.

However, the key to combating this new reality is to understand
who Trump actually is; to delve more into the GOP, and what the

goals really are from their end. Later on in the book, we will look at the similarities between both parties, and how they might compromise to find common ground.

DONALD TRUMP

Let us look at the president himself first – where he came from, how he got started, and who he is today. Perhaps by understanding the man himself, one can truly understand what he wants to achieve as president of the United States of America.

Donald Trump was born in Queens, New York on June 14th, 1946. He was a third-generation businessman, and after graduating with an economics degree, he took over his family's real estate business. Not long after, he started the Trump organization, and many other business ventures as well.

Donald Trump has gotten himself married a total of three times. Two of those marriages lasted over ten years, and neither of his ex-wives have anything bad to say about him. He has five children in total, all of whom are ambitious. Four of them have gone on to become successful business people. The fifth is currently excelling in school.

When Donald Trump became president, he decided to hand over his business to his two sons to avoid a conflict of interest between his business interests and higher office, particularly as to how those relate to foreign countries.

Trump had in fact expressed an interest in politics before he ever ran for president in 2016. He actually attempted to run in the 2000 campaign but did not make it very far, as he was not quite ready for the challenge at the time. He had too many minor controversies going on at the time due to bankruptcies and lawsuits over failing to pay contractors who had worked on his properties and for his businesses. However, in the 2016 election, he came out all guns blazing, and the rest, as they say, is history. He made it all the way to the White House, despite one of the most unorthodox campaigns the country has ever seen, despite frequent rage, spats with every and anyone, and policies that oozed controversy. Trump declared himself a nationalist and ran on a platform of eliminating illegal arrivals and building a wall. His campaign featured a number of simple yet direct slogans, such as build that wall, drain the swamp, and lock her up. There is still some level of uncertainty about whether Trump's victory was really because the right adored him, or because voters simply sought any means possible to make sure that his main rival, Hillary Clinton, did not take office.

Trump's presidency, which is now into its second year, has been full of controversy from day one. One of the many things he has done that has caused outrage, is to have withdrawn from virtually every climate change prevention agreement the US has ever entered into, including a number of measures Obama signed up to. He also instigated a travel ban on six predominantly Muslim countries. He retracted most of the Cuban Thaw, which was an agreement between the US and Cuba that made travel between the two countries legal once more, and he has tried, though as yet failed, to repeal and replace the Affordable Care Act. All of these things have deeply angered the left.

REAL ESTATE

Trump started out working for his father's company, which was called Elizabeth Trump and Son. They worked together to build their name on the back of middle-class rental properties. While that was the main early focus, they had business ventures elsewhere as well. These business ventures were often successful, such as when they took a foreclosed rental apartment building, revitalized it, and brought the occupancy rate up to 100% from 66%.

The company was later renamed the Trump Organization when Donald Trump took the helm, and his father became chairman of the board. The company seemed to thrive from 1971 onwards. However, it did attract controversy for a time. A large number of people claimed that the Trump organization refused to rent to African American tenants, and were extremely discriminatory against anyone who was not white. This attracted the attention of the justice system and from then on, they started renting to more minorities. No one can be sure about whether the allegations are one hundred percent true or not, and Trump himself has vehemently denied the claims.

LEGAL AFFAIRS and Bankruptcies

Trump and his businesses have been involved in around 3,500 legal cases, around 1,400 of which saw him as the defendant. The cases in which he was the plaintiff were mostly those where he was attempting to collect debts that had been wracked up by gamblers at his establishments. Often times these involved people who had the means but not the inclination to pay back the money they owed. They may have felt the Donald neither needed nor would miss the money. However, of those suits in which his case was solid, he only lost thirty-eight out of over four hundred.

Trump has had his businesses go bankrupt a total of six times, and although he has never filed for personal bankruptcy, it does appear as though he has taken the whole process to merely be a part of doing business. He has used bankruptcy at various times to wipe away debts, and while some of the bankruptcy proceedings were active, he was still able to successfully operate other businesses concurrently.

Trump's bankruptcies were mostly the result of over leveraging businesses in New York and Atlantic City. He made the error of placing too much stock in casinos that were built in towns with millions of places to gamble. He also put too much stock into hotels when there were many more affordable – and luxurious - options to choose from. Trump has often bragged about using bankruptcies to ease debt without having to ever pay it all back, claiming that it is "nothing personal, it is just business."

Now that you understand more about the man behind the desk let us move on to the Republican Party itself.

UNDERSTANDING THE GOP

A leader in the Democratic Party is a boss, in the Republican Party he is a leader.

— HARRY S. TRUMAN

☙❧

*T*he Republican Party has changed markedly in the nearly two hundred years it has been about. It started out as the Whigs party in protest of Andrew Jackson's "tyrannical" presidency. It started out as anti-slavery, and pro-public welfare. However, over its many years of its existence, things have indeed changed.

Over the years, the Republican Party has found itself, at different points, criticized for having supporters who might be deemed racist or for seeming to wish to minimize assistance to the poor. However, that might not be the fairest assessment, and might involve a mere fraction of supporters and may not be the belief of the party itself. While the GOP does seek welfare reform, it is not simply because they bear no concern for the less fortunate, but because they would prefer for the great American economy to last longer than it might do at current rates.

There are many things that the GOP would like to change about the current crop of legislative items, so let's take a look at some of them now, shall we?

- **Medicare reform:** The GOP wants to make Medicare pretty much disappear for the reason that without it, the economy will be in much better health. How can something that is gone continue to drain finances? However, a byproduct of such a measure is that millions would be left without affordable healthcare, which is a very big deal. As such, until a better – or reasonable - alternative can be put in place, the Medicare that we know today may be able to hold its ground and withstand the onslaught against its very existence.
- **Welfare reform:** The GOP wants to severely limit the amount of welfare that is being distributed by putting lifetime limits on what individuals can receive. They also want to make sure that every individual able to work is doing everything in their power to find a job. The goal of the GOP is to have every able individual standing on their own two feet and earning their own income, reserving welfare only for those people who truly are not able to work.
- **Economic reform:** At the heart of all of the changes the GOP wants to make, is economic reform. It wants the country to be the richest and most thriving in the world once again, and is trying to do everything in its power to make that happen. However, this means that some things have to change. Some hard decisions – and cuts – have to be made.

- **Immigration laws:** The GOP wants to crack down on immigration laws. It has already begun mass deportations of immigrants from Mexico who are perceived to be in America illegally, although that has become tied up in legal process. They have also shut down immigration routes from the Middle East to pretty much everyone who has not gone through a rigorous vetting process to get in. More security measures are in the works as we speak.
- **Tax reform:** This could go either way. The party is split on whether taxes should go up or down and for whom. The economy could benefit from higher taxes. However, most citizens cannot afford to pay higher taxes. Right now, a plan is being drawn up for tax reform.

Later on in the book, we will look at how compromise might be made on some of these issues.

DEMOCRATS AND LIBERALS

Americans' right to free speech should not be proportionate to their bank accounts.

— BERNIE SANDERS

❁

$\mathcal{N}$ow we turn our attention to the opposite side of the metaphorical wall. To the liberals and the Democrats. These two groups have often been grouped together by the media since the election, as they tried to band together to prevent Donald Trump from gaining the presidency. Ever since the election, Democrats and liberals have all been referred to as leftists and viewed as undesirables by Republicans, who themselves are also known as right-wing conservatives.

However, what if the two groups were not so different after all? What if there was a way that everyone could step a little closer despite their political differences, and understand that it matters not who is in the presidency, as long as they are working for the good of the country? Well, for that to happen one must first understand the ideals of the left and why they feel the way they do.

The left appears to be replete with millennials and supporters of such. These are either the people who were born into the recession or those who sympathize with the people who were born in the height of the recession. The economy might be said to have declined with the decline of the baby boomers, and it is up to the millennials to come along and pick up the pieces. This may make them seem a tad "bitter" against anyone from the right, because the right still views the world as it was thirty years ago, when you could get a job right out of high school, put yourself through college without a large loan, and still be able to buy a house as soon as you turned 21. However, nowadays, life is just not that easy.

Conservatives have nicknamed the left "snowflakes." They came up with this term because the left idolizes individuality, while still wanting everyone to be equal. While conservatives have tried to use this term as an insult, it has not quite turned out that way, because equality is something that America actually prides itself on. However, even though America is proud to be a country of equality, it is not always that equal, and this is what drives the left. It would dearly like to change that status quo.

At the head of the left during the presidential campaign was liberal candidate Bernie Sanders. Some people will argue that Hillary Clinton was its rightful head since she made it through the primaries, but in reality, Sanders was the most outspoken candidate there was. He continues to fight for the rights of those ordinary Americans from his place in the Senate.

There are many things that the left is criticized for, but their ideas may actually help the country. Perhaps if the left and right put their heads together, they may actually be able to come up with a plan to fix the economy while still helping the lower classes. Here are some of the things the left wants to fix.

- Less war: Unlike the conservative side of politics, the left feels that war is not quite the answer to every problem and that it is actually a huge drain on finances. The financial drain is true, as billions are spent each year on keeping the "war machine" running. If you were to ask a millennial today why we are at war, chances are that they would not even know the reason. This begs the question, why are Americans still fighting? Conservatives point towards terrorism, but what if when America recedes from the fight, the perceived enemy does back off? What if war was the main driver of terrorism? This, of course, may not be true, but it is worth a moment of thought.

- Tax the wealthy: Conservatives believe that not taxing the wealthy will allow them to spend more money on the economy and will create more benefits overall than taxing them. However, the numbers do not lie. If the wealthy were taxed, then the country could afford to keep the war going, along with all the welfare and assistance programs that are already in operation. The left feels that taxing the wealthy will help the economy, while still giving the wealthy plenty of money to spend on the economy as well.

- Lower poverty taxes: It seems like it is expensive to be poor. The wealthy benefit from all manner of tax cuts while those who are impoverished suffer from rising taxes. This makes little sense because it results in people not paying their taxes like they should. When they do not pay their taxes as they should, then the government fails to collect the money they need to help the economy. Reversing this situation, and taxing the wealthy instead can fix a lot of things.

- Flat rate loan APR: This is something that is not super important to the left, but could really help. Too many loan companies offer competitive APRs in order to entice borrowing. However, halfway through the said loans, the APR goes up, and the borrower has to scramble to cover rising interest in order to keep up with repayments and pay the loan off on time.
- Free healthcare: This is something that baffles the right. With the economy the way it is, how could the country ever afford to sustain free healthcare? It is simple. Too many hospitals are having to pay the litigation costs of going after people who haven't paid their bills, and most of the time they may not succeed because the person they're suing fails to make enough money to be able to pay them back. This leaves the hospital considerably out of pocket. Also, with free universal healthcare, pharmaceutical companies would be forced to make products more affordable, and cease the practice of price gouging on necessary products in their pursuit of large profits. If you have been watching the news, you probably know that the price of HIV medication went up 600 percent last year and the price of an EpiPen saw a 250 percent spike. This is because there would seem no reason to regulate the price of high importance goods, as the government doesn't take the hit for it and consumers will have to buy it any which way. In a world where the government is responsible for healthcare, these things can be regulated, and such price gouging would most likely not happen.
- Free college: This is another thing that the right sees merely as a money drain rather than a good thing. However, the way the left sees it, there are not a lot of skilled workers out there right now, because people can't even afford trade school, let alone an actual college degree. This is forcing

employers to employ workers in possession of less than a college degree, forcing them to spend more time and money training staff. Ultimately, that means less money will flow back into the economy. Also, many people who do go to college require grants and loans that never get paid back in any event. It just makes sense to make college free. That way those who do go wont be drowning in debt at the end of it, which means they'll have more money to spend and put back into the economy.

- Open door policy: The left wants to bring back the open door policy that America once had with Mexico. This concept brings outrage in pockets of the right, who fail to see the benefits of such an initiative. An open door policy would bring more Mexicans over who can work and pay taxes because they will not be illegal. This would put more money into the economy.

THE LEFT HAS some ideas that the right view as odious, and vice versa. Let's now look at how we can change that way of thinking, and get more people on the same page.

COMPROMISE AND UNDERSTANDING

Discourage litigation. Persuade your neighbors to compromise whenever you can. As a peacemaker the lawyer has superior opportunity of being a good man. There will still be business enough.

— ABRAHAM LINCOLN

*T*he most important thing you have to realize before trying to understand either side is that there is a generation gap that must be crossed. Things change, and if you keep a tight hold of the past, progress will never be able to succeed. Conservatives, one might say, are more nostalgic of the past, while millennials tend to look at the present situation or into the future.

These differences alone can cause a lot of head butting, however, once you learn to understand why someone thinks the way they do, there will be more room to find common ground.

Understanding The Other Side

Here is an exercise for you to try when you want to understand an opposing viewpoint. Take a deep breath and try to imagine yourself in the life of the other person. Take away all of your personal experience, and make your mind a fresh slate. Imagine you are living the life of the other person, as you go through all of his or her struggles and triumphs. This will make you more susceptible to listening to what they have to say. Who knows, you may even begin to agree with them. It just starts with you stepping out of your comfort zone and putting yourself in the other person's place.

Ok, now stop breathing deeply and let's get back to reality. When it comes to the left understanding the right, here is what you ought to know. The right came from a time where by hook or by crook you made things work even when they were broken. Back then things were a lot different and a lot less disposable than they are now. People worked hard every day, and wages were quite comparable to the cost of living. So that generation struggles to understand why wages, which seem so much higher today, still fall short of covering the cost of living. Most right-wing conservatives are at an age and situation that they do not have to worry about working minimum wage jobs. They have good paying jobs or are already retired with wonderful or at least sufficient pensions. This gives them a cushion of protection so that may never truly realize how much tougher things have become.

It is not simply that they do not care; it's just that they see things the way they were in the older days. Where if you worked hard enough you could achieve everything you wanted in life. It was waiting for you to just step up and grab. This generation wants people to experience pride in their life. They want people to work for what they have, which is why they want to do away with welfare for anyone who is not disabled. They struggle to understand the prevailing situation of some people who receive both welfare and income from a regular job because that can't survive on the salary alone. Opening the right's eyes to this issue may help solve a lot of problems.

15

When it comes to understanding the left, there is also a generational standpoint you have to take into consideration. The left has seen change in the world. More and more people have become tolerant of opposing viewpoints on a range of issues. The left wants America to be the melting pot it claims to be, rather than being the false advertisement for one that it is now. It also wants to try to keep up with the rest of the world in terms of advancements in caring for citizens. They see countries such as the UK with universal healthcare and free college, and they want American citizens to enjoy those same opportunities. The left fears that America will soon not be the most powerful country there is.

The truth is, the left may be right. Other countries have begun surpassing the US in terms of academia or in looking after its citizens, along with the passage of new rights for citizens. If this trend persists, the US might well be left in the dust figuratively unless it learns to catch up and unless it ceases to exist in the past. It is important that America moves forward, and stops hanging on to old ways. While the right wing conservatives have got it right that the economy was better then, things are changing. So how can there be compromise if the two groups think in totally opposite ways?

It is simple, actually. You just have to meet in the middle. There is always a middle somewhere, you just may have to travel a bit to get there. That is okay because the more you travel toward that middle ground, the more understanding of the other side you will have. It takes time, and it takes effort, but if you put in both of those things, you may walk away with a whole new view of the world. Who knows, you may even be able to make a difference.

How You Can Find a Middle Ground

First, look at all of the topics at hand, and view your stance on them. Once you figure out your opinion, then comes the hard part. Find similarities in the other side's opinions. They may be a little obscure, but there has to be something. You just have to dig. For example, say one person likes hamburgers, and another person likes hotdogs. The similarities are that both are meat products. It may seem like a bit of a stretch, but the similarities are there. Another small similarity is that both are often served at barbeques.

Finding small similarities, in the beginning, will help to find more similarities as time goes along. This makes it easier to find compromise. When one bases compromise on the similarities between ideas, then he or she can come up with a superb solution to any problem. You know what they say; two heads are better than one.

Let us look at all of the different ideas, and discuss possible solutions that might come closer to working for both. This will help to better understand both sides and maybe even find a mutual standpoint to follow.

Finding Common Ground in Politics

What are the similarities between the right and the left? This is a common question that many people find themselves asking when they hear that you can find common ground with those you view as opponents. However, there are more similarities than you might think.

Let us start with the obvious. Both parties want the economy to flourish. Both parties want to see America rise to greatness once more. Both parties want what is best for the American people. The only issue is that there are two totally different ideas on how to do that. So let us look at each issue, and try to find a common ground.

Issues

- Health: The left wants medical care for all, and the right wants standardized Medicare to go away. Where is the common ground here? Finances. Both want to change the current medical situation to help the economy. So which one is right? The truth is that it is not about who is right or wrong. It is about finding a solution that works. A possible solution could be that maybe everyone gets a basic medical plan, but after that, they have to pay for extra coverage. Make the extra coverage more affordable so that more people will choose to go for the extra coverage. This will put more money into the economy, or at least take a lot less out of it.

- Education: The left wants college to be free, while the right wants everyone to pay for college. Again, the issue comes back to finances. Currently, with the amount of people taking lower paying jobs just because they cannot afford to go to college, something obviously has to change. A compromise could be affordable college. Bringing back the college prices of the past to make college a more accessible option for everyone who wishes to attend. This will make higher paying jobs more accessible as well, and the more people that have more money, the more money they will spend. The more money that is spent, the more money that goes into and around the economy. It creates a ripple effect.

- Tax reform: Taxes are something that has been a bit of a bother ever since the country was founded. The Americans dumped hundreds of pounds of tea into the Boston Harbor over taxes. Now two hundred years later, America is still arguing over taxes, only this time, the taxes imposed by its own government. This leaves a lot of people angry. Let's face it, no one wants to or enjoys paying taxes. Unfortunately though, they are a necessary evil in the smooth running of the government. Taxing the wealthy would be a great way to help the economy. Reversing the current taxing standards would offer the lower class more money to spend and put into the economy, and may result in them having a lower need of federal assistance. The wealthy having higher taxes would put a lot more money into the economy, and they will still have plenty left over to spend.

- Immigration: This is a place where both sides butt heads immensely. The left believes that immigrants are essential to the economy, while the right believes that immigrants are a drain on the economy and blight on society. Let us look at the facts first. Many people from the right believe that illegal immigrants only come over to receive welfare. The truth is, illegal immigrants are not eligible to receive welfare, as they do not have proper identification. Maybe back when welfare was first introduced they were able to gain access to public assistance, but since identification became mandatory, no illegal arrival has been able to gain access to it. This means every dollar they spend at the store has been worked for. The only reason illegal immigrants are not a true help to the economy is that they are paid under the table, meaning their wages are not taxed. Deportation is expensive. Rather than deporting a million immigrants, a path to their citizenship should be made a lot easier to travel, so that people can emigrate to America, have the hope of becoming a citizen, and help out the economy.
- War: Of course, terrorism is a scary thing to think about. However, what if it was not as big of a problem as the right tries to make out it is. If America were to stop bombing other countries and killing their citizens, maybe they would stop trying to kill ours. A good compromise would be to withdraw from every war and try to make peace with all of the countries we are at war with. If a country refuses, then we obliterate them and move on. Okay, maybe obliterate is not quite the right sentiment, but you get the picture. Fighting a sixteen-year war is ridiculous, and the biggest drain on the economy that we have seen. It is time to cease the fighting or get it over with. Either way, if we only fought

wars for a short amount of time, and only when necessary, we could take the money that we are saving on war, and fix the national debt.

Here are some examples of compromise. From here you should be able to make your own thoughts on compromising on issues. The important thing is to realize that even if the ideas are different, the desire for an outcome is generally the same. No one wants to destroy the country, they just have different ideas on how to make it better. You too can come up with ideas, and who knows, maybe you can get your ideas heard and make a change. It is always worth a shot!

AFTERWORD

So there you have it, folks: A better understanding of both sides of the political playground that we are living in currently. If you are on either side, hopefully, you better understand those with opposing views and can learn to play together nicely. The more we work together, the better this world will be. The next time a friend or acquaintance offers an opposing position take a moment to pause. Hear him or her out. Empathize with his or her sentiments. Even noting some good points. And then put forward your own position. Debate and discuss the issues deeply and respectfully. You may not reach any sort of consensus, but you may just still be friends at the end. Or closer friends.

Hopefully, you enjoyed this little book on understanding Trump and the other side of the wall.

If you liked this book, and the contents that you read, please feel free to leave a review on Amazon. Thank you!

WANT MORE TRUMP?

Trump Revealed: A Great President?

OR EVEN MORE?

Understanding Trump: How to Survive the next 4 Years

Printed in Great Britain
by Amazon

25221351R00020